Living in Rural Communities

by Kristin Sterling

first step nonfiction

Lerner Publications · Minneapolis

Welcome to my **community.**

A community is a place
where people feel at home.

I live in a **rural** community.

Some people call rural communities the **country.**

There are many things to
see in the country.

Let's take a look around!

I see open land.

Some of the land is used
for farming.

I see farmers planting **crops.**

I see animals in a barn.

I see people riding horses.

I see long, empty roads.

I see my **neighbor.**

He lives in a house a few
miles away.

The country is quiet and pretty.

Do you live in the country?

There are different kinds of rural areas:

A reservation is land set aside for Native Americans.

A ranch is a large farm for
raising horses, sheep, and cattle.

A village is
a small group
of houses in
a rural area.

Rural Facts

 There are rural communities all around the world.

 In the past, farmers planted crops by hand. It took a long time and was very hard work. Most modern farmers use machines to plant their crops. They are able to have larger farms.

 Most rural Americans are not farmers. They work in other jobs helping people or making things.

Some rural areas have festivals to celebrate their history or a special time of year. More than 100,000 people went to the Cranberry Festival in Warrens, Wisconsin, in 2006.

 In the United States, about one in five people live in rural communities.

 Rural areas cover more than three quarters of the United States.

Glossary

 community – a place where people live together and feel at home

 country – an open area outside of towns or cities

 crops – plants the farmer grows and sells

 neighbor – a person who lives near your home

 rural – far from the city, a place with open land and few people

Index

The photographs in this book used with the permission of: © Index Stock Imagery/Stock Solution, cover; © Jim Cummins/CORBIS, pp. 2, 7, 22 (top); © Jamey Stillings/Stone/Getty Images, p. 3; © Walter Bibikow/JAI/CORBIS, pp. 4, 22 (bottom); © Jeff Greenburg/Alamy, pp. 5, 22 (second from top); © Ariel Skelley/CORBIS, p. 6; © Johner Images/Getty Images, p. 8; Peggy Greb/USDA, p. 9; © PhotoDisc Royalty Free by Getty Images, pp. 10, 22 (center); © Alvis Upitis/The Image Bank/Getty Images, p. 11; © Peter Correz/Stone/Getty Images, p. 12; Ken Hammond/USDA, p. 13; © Louis Schwartzberg/CORBIS, pp. 14, 22 (second from bottom); © Ross M. Horowitz/The Image Bank/Getty Images, p. 15; © Richard Price/Photographer's Choice/Getty Images, p. 16; © Anne Ackermann/Taxi/Getty Images, p. 17; © David McNew/ Getty Images, p. 18; © SuperStock, Inc./SuperStock, p. 19 (top); © Eugene Schulz, p. 19 (bottom).

Lerner Publications Company
A division of Lerner Publishing Group, Inc.
241 First Avenue North
Minneapolis, MN 55401 USA

For reading levels and more information, look up this title at www.lernerbooks.com.

Library of Congress Cataloging-in-Publication Data

Sterling, Kristin.
    Living in rural communities / by Kristin Sterling.
        p. cm. — (First step nonfiction - communities)
    Includes index.
    ISBN 978–0–8225–8599–2 (lib. bdg. : alk. paper)
    ISBN 978–0–7613–3988–5 (EB pdf)
        1. Sociology, Rural—Juvenile literature. 2. Rural conditions—Juvenile literature.
    3. Country life—Juvenile literature. 4. Communities—Juvenile literature.
    I. Title.
    HT421.S73 2008
    307.72—dc22   2007006365

Manufactured in the United States of America
8-42447-8848-6/3/2016